> CARING FOR MYSELF IS NOT SELF-INDULGENCE, IT IS SELF-PRESERVATION, AND THAT IS AN ACT OF POLITICAL WARFARE.
>
> —AUDRE LORDE
>
> BLACK FEMINIST LESBIAN ACTIVIST AND ICON

Library of Congress Control Number: 2025905839

Edited by Author Connections, LLC

GET YOUR ASSETS MOVING WITH THESE PRACTICAL TIPS AND RESOURCES

Learn valuable lessons from real-world stories

Tea is spilled and truth is served in these case studies that explore financial misfortune with silver linings, illustrate how to avoid money mistakes, and speak the language of boosting your financial savvy.

Take action to build a portfolio you can be proud of

Don't let procrastination, denial, and avoidance be the next step in your financial planning journey. These thought-provoking recommendations invite you to think deeply about what you need to live the most vibrant life you can.

Uncover smart money moves that can really pay off for you

Financial regulations, insurance benefits, and money markets are constantly changing. These action alerts give you details on how to take advantage of updated benefit policies and claim money you may be leaving on the table.

Explore additional planning resources

Look for QR codes that give you instant access to online financial tools, inclusive professional service directories, and comprehensive explanations of important financial, legal, and equal rights topics

BONUS! Scan THIS code now to learn more about the complimentary Take Pride in Your Money online companion course included with your book purchase.

CONTENTS

7 FOREWORD

11 INTRODUCTION

12 SECTION 1: WHY LGBTQ+ FINANCIAL PLANNING DEMANDS A DIFFERENT APPROACH

15 Money = Power

16 Fighting for Financial Equality

20 Paradoxical Politics

25 The "T" Also Stands for Trust

29 SECTION 2: HOW TO BUILD FINANCIAL STRENGTH IN A CHANGING LGBTQ+ LANDSCAPE

32 Who's Got Your Back? Align Yourself With Allies

35 Claim What's Yours: From Benefits to Beneficiaries

36 Marriage and Pensions

38 Marriage and Social Security

42 Marriage and Individual Retirement Accounts

43 Marriage and Inheritance

43 Life, Death, and Marriage

44 The Gay Divorcée

49 Pride & Protection:
The Importance of Insurance

49 Disability Coverage

50 Chronic/Critical Illness Coverage

51 Life Insurance Payouts

51 Medicare

52 Group Coverage

52 Medicaid

53 Trusts

53 Leveraging Long-Term Care Coverage

55 Caregiving in Our Community

57 "Gay-ging" in America: The Next Revolution

57 The Shifting Demographics of LGBTQ+ Aging

58 Exploring New Models of Communal Living

59 Left Out or Let In? The LGBTQ+ Aging Dilemma

63 Strengthening LGBTQ+ Bonds in Later Life

64 Estate Planning Ensures a Happy Ending

65 Power of Attorney

65 Wills & Trusts

66 Advanced Healthcare Directives

66 Beneficiaries & Titling

67 Guardianship

72 Empower Your LGBTQ+
Money to Ignite Change

72 Barriers, Behaviors & Biases, Oh My!

76 ESG & DEI: LGBTQ+ Values In Action

79 Confessions of A Client Whisperer

80 What's Your Money Mantra?

83 ABOUT THE AUTHOR

FOREWORD

Larry Kramer wrote this in a 2011 CNN article that listed ten realities of AIDS …

> *"Too many people hate the people that AIDS most affects—gay people and people of color. I do not mean dislike or feel uncomfortable with. I mean hate. Downright hate. Down and dirty hate."* [1]

EVERYTHING OLD IS NEW AGAIN

Nearly fifteen years have passed since he wrote this. It has been almost forty-five years since AIDS first appeared in the United States The same hatred is returning and growing stronger.

Hatred of transgender people.

Hatred of people of color.

Hatred of the Jewish community.

Hatred of immigrants.

Hatred of anyone identified as *other.*

The horrors of Project 2025 are becoming real. Trump, Musk, and their minions continue to steamroll the Constitution with their bloodless coup aided by a complicit Congress. Americans' financial

1 *"AIDS is a plague allowed to happen,"* by Larry Kramer, www.cnn.com. January 14, 2011.

security, freedoms, and democratic institutions and guardrails are being annihilated at lightning speed.

I am writing this in early 2025, and who knows how much more damage may be done to our economy and freedoms tomorrow? Next week? Next month?

> Abandonment of diversity, equity, and inclusion (DEI).
>
> Forced erasure of transgender people.
>
> Callous and inhumane treatment of immigrants and their families.
>
> Collapse of government institutions that protect us from fraud, corruption, disease, and abject poverty.
>
> The end of federally-protected marriage equality may now be a question of *when*, not *if*.

BACK TO THE FUTURE

I never imagined that after decades of fighting for LGBTQ+ rights, we would be at this point in our country's history.

In the early years of the AIDS epidemic, gay men faced strong hatred and rejection. They cared for each other because no one else would. They made sure their friends were treated with dignity. They memorialized those who died too young. All while also organizing, speaking up, and pushing back against lies, fear, and ignorance through a dark and frightening era.

That persistence of resistance is best captured in this quote by Dan Savage ...

> "*During the darkest days of the AIDS crisis, we buried our friends in the morning, we protested in the afternoon, and we danced all night. The dance kept us in the fight because it was the dance we were fighting for...*"

We gained power from that fight.

The power to claim what's rightfully ours.

The power to be resilient no matter what comes our way.

The power to OWN our power.

As we stand on the precipice of an Orwellian and dystopian United States built upon hatred, exclusion, and greed, the LGBTQ+ community must activate that hard-earned power to use our queer money to protect ourselves.

We can't count on institutions, laws, or corporations to have our backs. LGBTQ+ people have spent too long depending on the so-called "goodwill" of others. Political parties use us as a bargaining chip. Corporations slap on a rainbow when it's profitable. The legal system gives us rights one day and yanks them away the next.

Enough! It's up to us to demand and secure our own future.

There are growing calls to claim our "queer sovereignty" through economic self-determination—fostering LGBTQ+-owned businesses, financial networks, and community wealth-building to reduce reliance on heteronormative power structures. LGBTQ+ people could invest in education, media, healthcare, and economic systems controlled by the community.

We cannot afford to be passive observers. We've seen what happens when we do not take financial and legal precautions. In a hostile environment, discrimination, legal battles, and policy rollbacks can affect where we live, who we love, and how we retire.

KEEP DANCING UNTIL WE WIN

I wrote *Take Pride in Your Money* to teach proven financial strategies and share real-world stories from my 35 years of providing advice and advocacy to my LGBTQ+ clients.

However, I never thought that the need for this type of LGBTQ-specific financial education would be so vital and urgent in our rapidly devolving country and uncertain world.

Now, this book is a call to empower our queer dollars to protect ourselves, each other, and our community. Together, we can navigate these dark times.

> *"... It didn't look like we were going to win then, and we did. It doesn't feel like we're going to win now, but we could. Keep fighting. Keep dancing."*
>
> —Dan Savage

INTRODUCTION

I'm a passionate advocate for LGBTQ+ financial empowerment.

My life and career experiences have shaped my mission to help LGBTQ+ individuals and couples take control of their financial future and live their best life.

I'm a gay man who has been out of the closet since adolescence. My husband and I have been together for almost 40 years. The financial planning and investment advice field has been my professional focus for over three decades.

This book is for the LGBTQ+ community, and it also contains a lot of useful information for financial advisors, to help them understand and serve LGBTQ+ clients better.

WHY LGBTQ+ FINANCIAL PLANNING DEMANDS A DIFFERENT APPROACH

The first section of this book focuses on the political and societal challenges the LGBTQ+ community faces, and how they affect financial planning and security.

It's eye-opening to see the difficulties that LGBTQ+ people often face overlooked and underestimated. Many people seem unaware and others minimize the effects of legislative and judicial attacks on LGBTQ+ rights.

Some points I make will not be new to those of us in the LGBTQ+ community, but it could be a helpful education for others.

HOW TO BUILD FINANCIAL STRENGTH IN A CHANGING LGBTQ+ LANDSCAPE

Using real-world scenarios of how financial planning is concretely different for LGBTQ+ people, this book's section is designed to help LGBTQ+ people (and their financial advisors) take action to strengthen and protect their financial security.

SECTION 1:

WHY LGBTQ+ FINANCIAL PLANNING DEMANDS A DIFFERENT APPROACH

> **WHEN ALL AMERICANS ARE TREATED AS EQUAL, NO MATTER WHO THEY ARE OR WHOM THEY LOVE, WE ARE ALL MORE FREE.**
>
> ——BARACK OBAMA

Some people are skeptical about the financial security challenges facing the LGBTQ+ community, stating that focus on a minority is actually the cause of division and separation. With a dramatic rise in anti-LGBTQ+ legislation and hostilities throughout our country — especially towards transgender individuals —it is this hostility that is creating divisions.

Some will say, "What's the big deal? Now that there is marriage equality, everything is pretty much equal for all." While progress has been made, nothing could be further from the truth.

Sometimes a statement will have a negative edge to it …

"Why do we keep having to separate each other into these groups?"

"Everyone is the same under the law."

What many people do not understand, is that the United States Supreme Court has legalized some forms of anti-LGBTQ+ discrimination as "free speech."[2]

In fact, those who are forcibly separating us in this country are now clearly attacking LGBTQ+ people. They are arguing in court, and winning, that they don't have to serve LGBTQ+ people. They are arguing for legal separation. They are arguing for "special rights" to not have to adhere to anti-discrimination laws because they violate their religious beliefs. For example, thirteen states have passed religious exemption laws permitting adoption and foster care agencies to discriminate against LGBTQ+ children and youth in their care as well as LGBTQ+ and other potential parents.[3]

This peculiarity is something straight people don't experience.

---

2 Gay Rights vs. Free Speech: Supreme Court Backs Web Designer Opposed to Same-Sex Marriage, The New York Times, July 1, 2023.

3 Every Child Deserves A Family: *13 States Have Passed Discriminatory Adoption and Foster Care Laws That Harm Children.* https://everychilddeservesafamily.com/state-bills

I've heard people argue that LGBTQ+ rights are special rights, and it has sometimes been argued that minority groups have more rights than others. There appears to be more than a little hypocrisy here. Some people state that same-sex marriage is NOT the same as opposite-sex marriage, and so they state there is no discrimination in treating unlike things differently.

The LGBTQ+ community cannot be blamed for this division. LGBTQ+ people are under attack in an unprecedented number of legislative bills and laws. This directly affects financial planning and security.

MONEY IS POWER

Money is power, and we LGBTQ+ people must use it wisely for ourselves, our community, our non-profit organizations, and the products and companies we support.

> **I am an accredited investment fiduciary and I have a legal duty to always do what's in a client's best interest.**
>
> **You need to feel that same duty to YOURSELF.**

How you spend your money is like voting with your dollars.

You vote for certain businesses and services when you choose to spend your money there.

"Vote" for products and services that support you, and don't "vote" for companies or individuals who oppose you and your rights. As we have seen, companies which have supported Pride and DEI initiatives and policies have faced backlash from anti-LGBTQ+ forces. They need our continued support and affirmation to keep the momentum for change going.

Use your money to stand up for your values. Be educated and confident. Build a team of people who are on your side. Spend and invest your money with people who support and advocate for you.

When meeting with LGBTQ+ clients, there is ONE question that comes up almost every time. When they ask me for a referral — it could be to an estate planning attorney, a CPA, an assisted living facility, or any service — they ask: "Are they part of our community? Are they LGBTQ+-friendly?"

Of course, I refer clients to professionals who are culturally competent in dealing with LGBTQ+ issues and challenges. These referrals are often to straight service providers, yet I know with full trust that they are solid allies to our community.

That this question gets asked so often tells me that comfort level is an issue. People need that taken off the table so they don't have to worry about it.

Why is it that people ask this question? There are several reasons why...

- You don't want to be discriminated against.
- You don't want to be misunderstood.
- You don't want to feel that you're being judged, looked down upon, or that you're working with somebody who may not respect you and your values.

As a long-time openly gay financial advisor, I have dealt with all of these issues and am happy to share my strategies with you.

It's time to claim the power of your queer dollars.

FIGHTING FOR FINANCIAL EQUALITY

I get well-meaning comments from other financial advisors like, "I would love to get more LGBTQ+ clients. I have no problem with them." Not being biased against someone is not a qualification. It's a minimum expectation.

Taking pride in your money is not only about supporting those who support you. It is also about the opposite: Don't work with people who are working against you.

The historically conservative nature of the financial industry is unmistakable. It is changing over time, but the majority are still older white males, and conservative.

Although demographics are shifting, real-world experiences and perceptions do not demonstrate that women, LGBTQ+ people, and other marginalized populations are feeling welcomed, included, or even well-served. In 2023, 55% of LGBTQ+ Americans said they had been subject to discrimination within the financial services, banking, or investment industries.[4]

proactive pride

Don't be surprised by anti-LGBTQ+ laws or discriminatory court decisions. Don't be caught unprepared for hostile relatives, or a hostile boss or co-worker. The best thing you can do at times of uncertainty is to be prepared and proactive.

One good mental and emotional approach is to focus on your own well-being and what you can control.

How you manage your money is within your control.

4 September 2023: https://www.fool.com/research/lgbtq-money-study/

here's the tea

LEADING THE CHARGE FOR INCLUSION

In 2010, I was invited to attend a national financial services conference with all expenses paid, along with a family member—not just a guest, but specifically a family member. This was while marriage equality was heating up and there was not yet federal legal recognition of same-sex marriage.

I registered for this conference with Luis, my partner of 25 years, as my family member. They rejected his registration. I was told I could bring my brother, but not my husband.

The firm arranging the travel read the policy over the phone to me, but would not provide it to me in writing. I was told that the reason they couldn't have same-sex couples at sponsored company events had to do with all the different companies under one corporate umbrella, different corporate policies, and taxes. I believed them.

I said, "Okay then. I will take this on as a project to get this policy changed for the future." I researched domestic partnership benefit policies from other companies, to show how a more inclusive policy could be implemented. I brought various examples to the conference for the hosts' review, and told them that if they wouldn't accept my husband as a family member, he would still go with me as my guest, we would arrange our own flights, and he would stay in my room at the hotel. They told me that only registered guests would be welcome at conference events, so even if he was there, he wouldn't be able to attend any sessions or receptions.

The opening night was a gala dinner. When I checked-in at the registration table with Luis by my side, the tension was thick. We were mingling around outside the venue with other invited guests, waiting for the dinner to begin. When it started, everyone walked by us and we were not allowed in.

This wasn't a situation where we were forced to sit at the back of the bus—we weren't even allowed on the bus.

The next day, when I presented sample domestic partner policies from other companies, I was told by the company manager that if I thought I was going to change their policy I would be sorely disappointed. If this was about having differing company policies under a larger corporate umbrella and taxes, then surely with some reasonable effort, changes could be made.

After the conference, I followed up with the company manager to discuss their conference attendee policies. He refused to take my calls. Finally, I got a call back from the company's internal attorney with the manager also on the line.

This phone call was a personal triumph. Sometimes the words don't flow when you need them, and you finish an important conversation regretting that you didn't think to say certain things. Not this time. For twenty minutes, I berated them about lying to me and leading me down a fruitless path of hunting down inclusive corporate policies.

I had done my research and learned the real reason why they weren't interested in adopting more inclusive policies. Top leadership were conservative Christians and their president was a Campus Crusade for Christ board member.

They could have been honest. They could have said, "We are a conservative company and until the law changes, we have a policy that—whether you agree with it or not—is in place for now. David, we hope you will continue to work with us." They could have said anything along those lines and then let me make my decision.

Once marriage equality became federal law, that corporation changed its policy. I found out years later from a new employee there that my case had become somewhat famous at the time.

The time and energy to fight discrimination, potential loss of a job, unequal treatment, and ongoing threats to equal rights are all costs. It can affect choices of where to live and what profession to pursue. These are significant differences in financial planning that affect the LGBTQ+ community.

BOTTOM LINE

PARADOXICAL POLITICS: WELCOME TO "THE FREE STATE OF FLORIDA"

In my home state of Florida, Gov. Ron DeSantis signed into law the Protections of Medical Conscience Act, a law that went into effect on July 1, 2023. It allows any medical provider or insurer to deny care based on ethical, moral, or religious beliefs.[5]

This Florida law sets up another case where courts all too determined to carve out 'rights' for religious conservatives. Businesses can legally deny life-saving services to LGBTQ+ people or other minorities. It's no wonder that within the community, the law is known as the "Let Them Die Act."

5 The Florida Senate: CS/SB 1580 — Protections of Medical Conscience. https://www.flsenate.gov/Committees/BillSummaries/2023/html/3211

Florida is at the forefront of a nationwide attack on the rights of LGBTQ+ citizens.

- The Parental Rights in Education ("Don't Say Gay") law prohibits classroom instruction on sexual orientation and gender identity in all grades. This is empowering removal of LGBTQ+ and minority-themed books from school libraries.
- The Stop Wrongs to Our Kids and Employees Act ("Stop WOKE")—redubbed the Individual Freedom Act—prohibits schools and businesses from teaching certain concepts related to race, racism, and privilege.
- Smaller businesses like restaurants have been targeted for presenting drag shows.
- The state of Florida has removed LGBTQ+ tourism outreach information from its tourism website. DeSantis even took away the freedom of local communities to light up bridges in rainbow colors for June's Pride Month. He cynically announced this change as honoring "Freedom Summer" by requiring that only red, white, and blue colors could be used to light bridges during the summer season.

In 1775, Samuel Johnson stated, "Patriotism is the last refuge of a scoundrel." One could argue that is still true today.

Many conservative politicians talk hypocritically about small government, fewer regulations, and more 'freedom'.

Freedom for whom?

Collectively, this is all demonization and dehumanization of the LGBTQ+ and other minority communities. These policies cause real and tragic harm to current and future generations. More than ever, this is when our community must support organizations that provide safe (and life-saving) spaces for our youth and families, fight back in the courts, and push back against dangerously regressive laws.

BIGOTRY DISGUISED AS CONCERN: UNMASKING HARMFUL LEGISLATION

There has long been the concept of "plausible deniability," meaning that you can justify something terrible or even illegal by credibly denying something (such as intent, level of involvement, resulting consequences, etc.). Perpetrators do the dirty work while planning to plead ignorance about their actions and the damages caused. These lies are also used to make something horrible look more reasonable, giving supporters some cover to hide.

Many anti-LGBTQ+ bills are shrouded in plausible deniability, with statements like ...

"This law is just to protect children from something inappropriate."

"This law is just to stop corporations from having too much power."

"This law is just to protect against extremist ideology."

In response, another statement comes to mind ...

"We call BS."

These words from Emma González ring true for the justifications above. Emma is one of the courageous Parkland High School students fighting for gun reform after 17 friends and teachers were murdered in a mass shooting there in 2018.

LGBTQ+ people are back to being demonized as "groomers" — a term I thought had been retired after decades of equal rights advances. I'm old enough to remember Anita Bryant's anti-LGBTQ+ crusades in the 70s, when we were attacked as "recruiters." She said that since we can't reproduce, we have to recruit. "Save Our Children" was the cry.

History is repeating itself. It's never about the children. It's about attacking people you don't like and using children as an excuse, even as a weapon, and even personalizing it to say that "they" are coming for YOUR children.

Decent people need to fight against all of this. Many Americans have this naïve notion that "it can't happen here." Until it does.

We weren't going to have a global pandemic with over a million Americans dead. But we did.

We would never have an insurrection and coup attempt to overthrow a free and fair election with seditionists violently invading the United States Capitol during the actual vote count—with slates of fake electors from seven key states ready to overturn their states' popular votes. But we did.

These attacks on our democracy are relentless. What comes next? Who will be targeted?

MARRIAGE RIGHTS COULD BE NEXT

When the United States Supreme Court overturned Roe v. Wade, I was outspoken about LGBTQ+ rights and marriage equality coming under the gun next. I think most people are still in denial about what can happen. Some are relying on statements by Supreme Court justices themselves, that overturning Roe v. Wade was a singular decision not affecting other decisions. The Supreme Court said the same thing in the recent case allowing a website designer to refuse service to LGBTQ+ couples.

The court specifically mentioned in overturning Roe v. Wade that other laws, including marriage equality (the Obergefell decision), should also be "revisited." One justice, Clarence Thomas, specifically called for overturning Obergefell, and Justice Alito previously called for it to be overturned in a scathing opinion regarding Kim Davis, a Kentucky official who brazenly broke the new law and refused to grant marriage licenses to LGBTQ+ couples.

Congress passed the Respect for Marriage Law in an attempt to get ahead of any contradictory Supreme Court decision. Enough

Republicans voted in favor of the new law for it to pass, and President Biden signed it into law.

The vast majority of Republicans, however, voted against the law, and often made excuses that it burdens religious liberty. Others were more openly hostile and felt no need to hide behind religious liberty arguments. They made comments about same-sex marriage being a threat to society.

A Republican majority in both houses of Congress and a Republican president in power could repeal the Respect for Marriage Act and "let the states decide." That could happen even before any Supreme Court decision.

There is no substitute for marriage and the rights it offers. If the Supreme Court were to overturn Obergefell at some point, we would be at the mercy of Congress to not also overturn the Respect for Marriage Act.

Speaker of the House Michael Johnson literally made a living as an attorney for Alliance Defending Freedom, a designated hate group[6] that is dedicated to recriminalizing sexual acts between consenting LGBTQ+ adults and undoing marriage equality in our country.

More and more extreme laws are being passed and ending up in the courts. I fully expect that the LGBTQ+ community will prevail in the long run, but the question is how much damage can be done in the meantime?

One of the best ways to fight back against attacks and threats is to align your money with your values and be sure you are financially protected for whatever the future may bring.

---

6 https://www.splcenter.org/fighting-hate/extremist-files/group/alliance-defending-freedom

THE "T" ALSO STANDS FOR TRUST

Transgender. Gay. Bi. Queer. Straight. Questioning. Two-Spirit. Non-binary. Intersex.

Visibility matters. Identity matters. Because *you* matter.

It's not enough to say, "I treat everyone the same." Because not everyone is the same—and pretending otherwise erases lived experience. In financial planning, this is more than philosophy. It's practice. And it can be the difference between financial freedom and financial fragility.

Let's talk trust. If you're transgender, chances are you've had to fight harder than most for basic recognition—let alone respect. So when it comes to finances—one of the most personal, sensitive areas of life—you deserve more than just tolerance.

You deserve professionals who get it.

Historically, the financial industry hasn't felt like a safe or welcoming place. It's still dominated by straight, white men. As of the latest data, over 76% of financial advisors are white. More than two-thirds are male.[7] It's no wonder transgender individuals often feel alienated—or flat-out rejected.

But here's the truth: Trust is the foundation of any good financial plan. And trust requires representation, empathy, and understanding.

MONEY IS PERSONAL. SO LET'S TALK ABOUT YOU

Imagine this: You meet with a financial advisor. You want to talk about saving for top surgery. Or how to financially prepare for a name and gender marker change. Maybe you need to figure out insurance

7 https://datausa.io/profile/soc/personal-financial-advisors#demographics

options for hormone therapy. But instead, you feel the advisor flinch. Or they ask invasive, irrelevant questions. Or worse—nothing at all.

Without a strong, safe relationship between client and advisor, it's impossible to create a truly effective financial plan. Advisors need to understand more than just markets and math. They need to understand you. Your identity. Your lived experience. Your goals.

Being "inclusive" isn't just the right thing to do. It's essential for doing this job well.

THE FINANCIAL TERRAIN: TOUGHER THAN IT SHOULD BE

Let's not sugarcoat it—being transgender in America comes with steep financial challenges.

A 2022 study[8] by the National Center for Transgender Equality[9] found the unemployment rate among transgender individuals was five times the national average. Over one-third live in poverty.

And it's not just about income. It's about access. It's about being blocked from opportunity at every turn.

Here's how that plays out:

- **Employment Discrimination:** Despite legal progress, workplace discrimination persists. Many transgender individuals are underemployed—or excluded entirely.
- **Healthcare Costs:** Transition-related care can be lifesaving. It's also often expensive. Even with insurance, out-of-pocket costs can cripple a budget.

8 *Early Insights: A Report of the 2022 United States Transgender Survey,* Sandy E. James, Jody L. Herman, Laura E. Durso, and Rodrigo Heng-Lehtinen, February 2024

9 https://transequality.org/what-we-do

- **Legal Expenses:** Changing your name and gender marker isn't free. Legal fees and paperwork add up, and many can't afford the price tag of being correctly identified.
- **Housing Instability:** Transgender people are far more likely to experience homelessness and housing insecurity. Without stable housing, financial planning becomes a pipe dream.
- **Family Rejection:** No financial safety net. No emergency backup. Many trans people are cut off from familial support the rest of us take for granted.

These challenges aren't theoretical—they're daily realities. And they demand a financial system and professional support network that's ready to rise to the occasion.

BUILDING A BETTER FUTURE—TOGETHER

So how do we change the game?

It starts with financial advisors who don't just serve transgender clients—they *advocate* for them. Who take the time to understand the nuance, the roadblocks, and the strategies that make financial planning work for transgender lives.

Here's what that advocacy looks like in practice:

- **Insurance Navigation:** Understanding what plans cover gender-affirming care—and how to minimize out-of-pocket costs—is critical. Trans clients need advisors who know how to decode this maze.
- **Smart, Value-Based Investing:** Many transgender individuals want to invest in companies aligned with their values. ESG (Environmental, Social, Governance) screening lets you invest without compromising who you are. Your dollars can reflect your dignity.
- **Strategic Budgeting:** Whether it's saving for medical procedures, legal changes, or an emergency fund, tailored

budgeting strategies empower trans clients to set—and achieve—their financial goals.

- **Creating Safe Space:** Above all, financial professionals must create an environment where transgender clients can speak freely. No shame. No hesitation. Just real talk and real help.

This isn't just about individual advisors. Financial institutions, employers, and policymakers have a moral and economic imperative to do better.

They must:

- Enforce nondiscrimination protections.
- Offer comprehensive healthcare coverage.
- Provide financial literacy tools tailored to transgender communities.
- Fund programs that fight poverty in transgender communities.

You shouldn't have to fight for the right to exist and for financial security. But here we are. And until systems change, the path forward is carved by people—professionals who care, who advocate, who get it.

The financial planning journey can be empowering, affirming, and even joyful when it centers your truth. You are not a financial risk. You are a financial force.

SECTION 2:

HOW TO BUILD FINANCIAL STRENGTH IN A CHANGING LGBTQ+ LANDSCAPE

“

THE FIGHT FOR LGBTQ+ RIGHTS HAS LONG BEEN FRAMED AS A STRUGGLE FOR INTEGRATION, RECOGNITION, AND PROTECTION WITHIN EXISTING POWER STRUCTURES. BUT WHAT IF THOSE STRUCTURES ARE NO LONGER WILLING OR CAPABLE OF ENSURING OUR DIGNITY AND SAFETY? THEN IT IS NO LONGER ENOUGH TO ADVOCATE WITHIN THE SYSTEM. WE MUST BUILD OUR OWN.

——FABRICE HOUDART

”

Many view financial planning as an extremely personal and private matter. Sharing sensitive details about financial assets — or lack thereof — earnings, attitudes about money, life goals, dreams, and how assets are to be left to loved ones with a professional you barely know may cause anyone to feel uncomfortable or even embarrassed.

For LGBTQ+ individuals and couples, the discomfort and unease of the experience are often compounded. They may be reticent to disclose their sexual orientation or share the full nature of their family relationships. This is especially prevalent among older lesbians and gay men who may have struggled with coming out late in life after living in the closet for years.

In the course of decades helping LGBTQ+ clients, I have witnessed first-hand the impact of many of these concerns—both in my own personal life and through the real-world experiences of my clients and their families. I take pride in sharing practical solutions to help you make more empowered financial and life-planning decisions.

here's the tea

"YOU KNOW HE'S A HOMO"

When I first met an older man who was referred to me, he was very closeted. He came to a party that I hosted with my husband but he never came out to me, even though he was with another older gentleman.

The next day, he called me and said something cryptic. "It's like, oh, you know, kind of what I've always wanted, you and your partner." I realized he was coming out to me, that he was a gay man, too. We started working together and ended up having lunch together every other Saturday for seven years. I slowly took over managing his accounts.

At some point I reached out to his sister, his closest living relative. When possible, I always like to get the family involved. I asked him, "Can I speak to your sister about your accounts? Is there anything, you know, that's private that you don't want me to say?"

He answered, "You can talk to her about anything, all my accounts, but please don't talk about my personal situation." By 'personal situation,' he meant I should not discuss him being gay.

I called her, and we hit it off. We had a great conversation. Towards the end, she said, "You know he's a homo."

I laughed, thinking, Who talks like that anymore? But that's age. I wanted to say something, something like, "Well, so am I." But I thought that would almost be like outing him. I wanted to respect his privacy and he had specifically asked me not to discuss this with his sister. It was still just too private. It's been that way all their lives and they still want to keep it that way. They are not the only family with an elephant-in-the-room secret that looms between them. It is still an issue for that generation.

WHO'S GOT YOUR BACK? ALIGN YOURSELF WITH ALLIES

Unless you are living in a "gay bubble," our community still has to deal with judgment, ignorance, and disrespect relating to gender and sexual identities.

These experiences can deeply impact LGBTQ+ people and leave them with feelings of mistrust. This makes it even more important to seek out trusted professionals — from doctors and lawyers to financial planners — who are allies and advocates acting in the best interests of the LGBTQ+ community. Having a team of culturally competent professionals on your side is invaluable. I stated why in an interview with the *South Florida Business Journal:*[10]

> *'Companies shouldn't be afraid to promote DEI because political rhetoric is not often reflective of their workforce or clientele,' said David Treece, head of Miami-based investment advisor Treece Financial Group and an LGBTQ+ activist. Workers in his industry are overwhelmingly older white men, 'but clients of all types need investment and wealth management services,' he added.*

If you want to know whether an advisor or someone referred to you is LGBTQ+-friendly, ask someone who knows. Someone attuned to the financial planning needs of our community wouldn't refer you to someone who supports an anti-LGBTQ+conservative agenda.

I have a fantastic network of attorneys and accountants, plus many others in a wide range of fields that I can confidently refer to my LGBTQ+ clients without them having to worry about coming out of the closet and getting some weird reaction. I can take that whole issue off the table for them. And you know what? My biggest referral partners are NOT LGBTQ+, but they're allies of our community who are firmly on our side.

---

10 "Companies grapple with DEI pushback: Political debate endangers workplace inclusion efforts", *South Florida Business Journal,* August 3, 2023. https://www.bizjournals.com/southflorida/news/2023/08/03/companies-grapple-with-dei-political-pushback.html

More than likely, a LGBTQ+-allied professional will have proven experience in:

- Successfully helping other LGBTQ+ individuals, couples, and families.
- Listening, to understand your individual needs and concerns.
- Partnering with resources that provide welcoming and inclusive services.
- Advocating in your best interests to overcome difficult challenges.
- Promoting inclusivity, equity, and respect for their clients in the wider community.

All of the above points are at the heart of my mission to empower the financial savvy of LGBTQ+ clients and the providers who serve them. My commitment includes the broker-dealer I partner with. Cetera Advisors LLC is deeply dedicated to DEI initiatives. I was honored to serve on the company's first Inclusion & Impact Council.

My long-term commitment to building LGBTQ+ community and connections in South Florida inspired me to found La Vida Pride. This complimentary, secure, member-driven online community offers courses, resources, and a directory of vetted allied professionals to help older LGBTQ+ adults continue aging out loud, proud, and prepared. My goal is to supplement other national guides with more peer-to-peer input from the LGBTQ+ community who utilize these service providers.

ACCESS COURSES, RESOURCES, AND CONNECTIONS TO CONTINUE LIVING OUT LOUD, PROUD, AND PREPARED

Scan this QR code to join the La Vida Pride™ eCommunity.

FIND OUT WHERE EMPLOYERS STAND ON LGBTQ+ EQUALITY

Scan this QR code to search companies, municipalities and healthcare facilities to see how they rate on HRC's Corporate, Municipal and Healthcare Equality Indices.

DISCOVER LGBTQ-ALLIED RESOURCES IN YOUR STATE

Scan this QR code to search the National Gay & Lesbian Chamber of Commerce's state-by-state affiliate member listings.

CLAIM WHAT'S YOURS: FROM BENEFITS TO BENEFICIARIES

Marriage equality has been one of the most significant financial planning changes for LGBTQ+ couples in our lifetime.

Unfortunately, the biggest potential threat is the loss of marriage rights.

I personally remain optimistic that marriage equality will remain the law of the land in all fifty states due to overwhelming public support. Of course, a solid majority of Americans also supported Roe v. Wade, but that didn't matter. It is best to always be prepared for whatever may or may not happen.

Marriage is relatively new for LGBTQ+ couples. Knowledge of rights and implications is still being discovered by same-sex couples transitioning from long-term partnerships to legal marriage. Many older LGBTQ+ people never thought they would get married because they never imagined they would have the legal right to do so.

All LGBTQ+ couples need to first answer the critical question:

Should we even get married?

Some long-term couples feel like it minimizes all their years together if they head to the altar and get legally married. For years they've told themselves that marriage is "just a piece of paper." That perception is far from the truth when it comes to receiving benefits, naming beneficiaries, and planning for financial security.

Another difference is the identity change that same-sex couples go through after getting married. Your status changes—both legal status and your status in society. Instead of referring to your "partner" or some other less clear term, LGBTQ+ people can now refer to their legally married spouses as their "wife" or "husband." LGBTQ+ people who have gotten married often say that they felt deeply transformed. Their relationship has been legally validated.

Heterosexual people know the difference, too. It is clearer to them, too, when a gay man refers to his husband or a lesbian refers to her wife.

MARRIAGE AND PENSIONS

The relative newness of marriage equality led long-term couples to make choices based on the expectation of always being legally single. For example, a spouse might have taken a pension based on a single-life payout as opposed to a joint-life payout. Think about the difference this makes for a same-sex couple. When the spouse with that single-life pension payout dies, the pension ends. One Social Security check will be lost, too.

here's the tea

THE PAIN OF A PENSION LOST

A gay man who worked at a big-name automobile company married his husband before same-sex marriage was legally recognized, which complicated things when he retired. Because his marriage wasn't acknowledged, the only option he had was to choose a single-life pension, which only covered him.

Years later, the company decided to offer retirees a lump sum payout to get these pensions off their books. With marriage equality now in place, his advisor wanted to see if there was a way to switch the payout to a joint-life pension, which would provide for both spouses. After weeks of back-and-forth with the company, the response came in: changing the payout structure wasn't possible. Once a pension type is chosen, it's usually set in stone.

That left the client with a tough choice. Should he keep his single-life pension as a steady monthly income? Or should he take the lump sum payout instead? The numbers were one thing, but there were bigger issues to think about.

If he stuck with the single-life pension and something happened to him suddenly, the payments would stop completely and his husband would be left with nothing.

With a lump sum, they could create an investment strategy that not only mimicked the pension's monthly income but could also include a death benefit for his spouse.

In the end, they decided the lump sum was the best way to go. It gave them the flexibility to ensure income for both of them and provided financial confidence knowing the husband would be taken care of.

MARRIAGE AND SOCIAL SECURITY

Similar to pension decisions, many LGBTQ+ couples have missed out on Social Security benefits because of the previous lack of marriage rights.

A long-time couple might never have considered Social Security spousal benefits because their relationship existed before marriage was an option. The same is true of Social Security survivor benefits, where a former partner passed away before marriage equality.

This applies also to Social Security divorced spousal benefits, because of the rule requiring a marriage to have lasted ten years before being eligible to claim divorced spouse benefits. If a relationship ended where they would have been married for ten years or longer, but weren't married due to the lack of marriage rights at the time, divorced spouse benefits are lost.

This also applies to divorced spouse survivor benefits. (Spousal benefits are generally 50% of the spouse's benefit when they are alive and then generally convert to 100% as SURVIVOR benefits upon the spouse's passing). The loss of these benefits is lifelong and significant.

benefit alert!

You may now be eligible to apply for Social Security benefits based on a former same-sex relationship due to two class-

action lawsuits. You can file a claim for benefits if you did not meet the marriage requirements because of an unconstitutional state law. This is potentially huge for many people, and it is another glaring example of a giant difference regarding LGBTQ+ financial planning.

The former Trump administration kept these class action cases tied up in courts with appeals. The Biden administration stopped the appeals and opened the ability of same-sex couples to claim benefits. This has been another extended fight for equal treatment under the law even years after the Obergefell marriage equality decision.

The Social Security Administration has a rule that a couple must have been married for nine months for a spouse to be able to claim survivor benefits. With the new court ruling, if a same-sex couple was prevented from being married for at least nine months by unconstitutional laws barring same-sex marriage, the surviving spouse will now be able to claim Social Security survivor benefits.

here's the tea

SECOND CHANCE FOR THE SURVIVOR

This case involves a same-sex couple who got married in California. Unfortunately, one of the husbands passed away unexpectedly before they had been married for nine months. When the surviving husband applied for Social Security survivor benefits, his claim was denied because of the "nine-month rule," which requires a couple to be married for at least nine months before one spouse is eligible to receive benefits.

This rule is meant to prevent fraud, but it's had an unfair impact on many couples who married later in life due to lack of marriage equality in the past. Because of this, the surviving spouse was initially left without the benefits he would have received if their marriage had been legally recognized earlier.

Since changes to Social Security guidelines now allow people to reopen their survivor benefit claim, he did so. That allowed him to receive monthly benefits going forward, but also meant that he could be eligible for retroactive payments going back to the time of his spouse's death.

The Social Security Administration has issued guidance and instructions on how to proceed. A potential claimant should call the Social Security Administration at 800-772-1213 or contact your local Social Security office.

What do you need to prove you would have been eligible for benefits?

The Social Security Administration states they will consider all available evidence of the circumstances that result in the couple being married for less than nine months when the spouse died. Here are some questions they may ask a surviving spouse in making the determination:

- *Did the law of the state where the ceremonial marriage occurred prohibit same-sex marriages until less than nine months before your deceased spouse's death?*
- *Would you have been married to your deceased spouse for at least nine months if a state law did not prohibit same-sex marriage?*
- *Did you live together? If yes, for how long?*
- *Did you own property together?*
- *Did you inherit from the deceased based on a will?"*

What if you never got married, even ceremonially? Social Security says, "We will consider all available evidence of the circumstances that resulted in the couple not being married when their partner died." Here are some questions they may ask a surviving partner in making the determination:

- *Would you have married if you were not prohibited from doing so?*
- *What date would you have married if you were not prohibited from doing so?*
- *Did you own property together?*
- *Did you live together and for how long?*
- *Did you own property together?*
- *Would you have been otherwise eligible to marry if the law had not barred same-sex couples from marriage?*

The Social Security Administration provides many other sample questions for consideration. Scan this QR code to review them.

A good financial advisor should be able to explain how these benefits are earned, calculated, and claimed. However, it is up to the Social Security Administration to make a final determination.

Many financial advisors aren't aware that LGBTQ+ couples who were never legally married might be able to file for Social Security benefits. This is another advantage of working with an advisor who serves and supports the LGBTQ+ community.

Social Security spousal and survivor benefits can add up to hundreds of thousands of dollars over a lifetime, and same-sex couples should not miss out on this money if eligible.

BOTTOM LINE

MARRIAGE AND INDIVIDUAL RETIREMENT ACCOUNTS

Marriage confers over a thousand rights. One of the biggest that affects a couple's financial security is the ability of a spouse to inherit an individual retirement account (IRA) as though it were his or her own.

If you are not legally married, your beneficiary is a "non-spouse," and falls under non-spouse rules. The biggest difference is that a non-spouse beneficiary must liquidate an IRA over ten years. A same-sex partner who is not legally married and inherits an IRA cannot postpone required minimum distributions or combine it with his or her own IRA.

They cannot leave it alone and let it grow for their own retirement. They must begin liquidating the IRA the year after the partner passes away, and then it must be completely emptied by the end of the tenth year. There are no 10% IRS penalties for these withdrawals if you are under age 59 ½, because these withdrawals are required.

Compare that to spousal beneficiary options:

1. The surviving spouse can set up an inherited IRA, begin withdrawals, and then convert it to a spousal IRA after age 59 ½ to avoid a required minimum distribution (RMD), then not touch it until their own required withdrawal start date, which is now being phased in for some people to begin as late as age 75.
2. The spousal IRA benefit includes the ability to make spousal contributions. You must have earned income to be able to contribute to an IRA unless you are married. If you are working but your spouse is not, you can make contributions not only for yourself, but contributions on behalf of your spouse in a spousal IRA owned by your spouse.

here's the tea

A spousal IRA beneficiary can leave that money to grow possibly for decades. A non-spouse beneficiary cannot leave the IRA for even one year. Withdrawals must begin the next year after the date of death. At the end of ten years, a spousal IRA might have grown substantially. At the end of ten years, a non-spousal IRA must have a ZERO balance.

MARRIAGE AND INHERITANCES

There can be a lost financial legacy for many LGBTQ+ couples where benefits could have been claimed by one partner for a pension, Social Security, spousal IRAs, and even lost inheritances in situations where estate planning documents, proper titling of assets, or naming of beneficiaries was not done.

For many older LGBTQ+ people, this is a lost legacy and one of many factors that can lead to LGBTQ+ people having a lower overall net worth than their straight counterparts.

LIFE, DEATH, AND MARRIAGE

Death certificates with a cause of death are generally private and only available to immediate family members or named beneficiaries. There are other short-form death certificates that do not list a cause of death, which are public.

If you are NOT legally married, you may not be able to get a death certificate that includes the cause of death for a partner. You would need this for a life insurance claim, although by being a beneficiary, you have a verifiable interest in getting a death certificate with a cause of death.

THE GAY DIVORCÉE

Divorce is a difficult life transition to navigate—no matter the genders of the spouses. There are countless repercussions, including the logistics of dividing assets, custody of children, and other legalities of separation.

First comes love. Then comes marriage. When comes divorce?

Marriage equality didn't become fully legal until the United States Supreme Court's Obergefell v. Hodges case in 2015. Since then, over 750,000 LGBTQ+ couples[11] have tied the knot.

In the push for equal rights, people focused on legalizing marriage equality and didn't think about the divorce process. The overall divorce rate of first marriages in the United States is 43% (60% for second marriages and 73% for third marriages)[12]. Recently, the gay divorce rate has also risen. In late 2023, Google searches for "gay divorce" nearly doubled.

This trend shouldn't be surprising since the average first marriage in the United States lasts about eight years[13] before ending in divorce. LGBTQ+ couples may simply be catching up to their opposite-sex counterparts.

Divorce rates are lower for LGBTQ+ couples than opposite-sex couples, but there are differences within the LGBTQ+ community.

---

11 https://www.census.gov/newsroom/stories/lgbt-pride-month.html

12 https://www.forbes.com/advisor/legal/divorce/divorce-statistics/#key_divorce_statistics_in_2024_section

13 https://www.forbes.com/advisor/legal/divorce/divorce-statistics/#key_divorce_statistics_in_2024_section

Lesbian couples are twice as likely to divorce[14] than gay male couples. This may have several explanations, including:

- Many lesbian couples enter into marriage more hastily and some end up regretting their decision.
- Lesbian couples usually marry later in life compared to gay male couples. They may also be more likely to have been previously married. This could potentially lead to a higher risk of divorce for lesbian couples.
- Women are less likely to tolerate cheating from their partner. They often cite infidelity as the main reason for divorce. This happens more frequently than it does for men.

The Not-So-Fabulous Aspects of LGBTQ+ Divorce

Couples in LGBTQ+ marriages face unique financial and legal challenges when getting a divorce.

Differences are more likely for LGBTQ+ couples given that the maximum length of their legal marriage can only be nine years. A relationship may be decades long and include previous civil unions or domestic partnership agreements, but ambivalence within the legal system and state laws can complicate a divorce.

There is no question that bias within the legal system is a real threat to a fair outcome. Many judges all the way up to the Supreme Court have shown open anti-gay bigotry and bias to religious arguments against gay people and against equal protection under the law. The mere risk of facing this bias or a protracted appeal due to an unfavorable outcome discourages fighting for equality that straight people take for granted.

Each state has its own laws. People who entered civil unions or domestic partnerships before same-sex marriage was legal may face challenges because of varying state laws. For example, if a same-

14 https://mediate.com/lgbtq-couples-and-divorce-trends/

sex couple married in one state but later moved to a different state, obtaining a divorce could be more difficult.

Property Division

The duration of a marriage significantly impacts how assets are divided. If the couple hasn't been married long, there's a chance that a spouse may not be eligible for financial support, or the couple may not reach an agreement regarding real estate and shared assets.

For same-sex couples who lived together before marriage became legal, there's no guarantee that you'll walk away from the marriage with anything your spouse bought before you were legally married.

Spousal Support

Alimony payments—spousal support—can be complicated in LGBTQ+ divorces when couples partnered before marriage equality. This is because the length of time they lived together before marriage can impact the alimony arrangement. LGBTQ+ couples in a long-term relationship before marriage may have a more complex alimony situation to navigate. Also, the length of some marriages is harder to determine based on past legal restrictions.

In some states, a spouse may ask the judge to award "palimony" (financial support for unmarried partners), based on the years the couple spent living together before they legally married.

Predicting the outcome of a spousal support case is difficult because judges have a lot of flexibility in their decisions. Because of this and varying alimony laws between states, seeking legal help from an alimony attorney is key to understanding your rights and benefits.

Child Support Payments and Custody Agreements

In 2017, the United States Supreme Court extended the Obergefell decision to other benefits of marriage, including parentage. Adoption by married same-sex couples was made legal in all United States

states. If a mother has a child through assisted reproduction while married, her wife will be recognized as the child's other parent. This means that the child will have two legal parents.

If the children of an LGBTQ+ couple are legally adopted by both spouses, support and custody processes are the same as those for heterosexual couples.

In other cases, although parents may have raised a child equally, this doesn't mean they have equal rights to the child as they would in an opposite-sex relationship. Legal definitions of gaining custody or even court ordered visitation rights can be an obstacle when one parent is not the child's biological or adoptive parent.

Parental recognition laws vary by state. It is crucial to research the laws in your state. This will help you understand your rights, reduce legal fees, and identify potential challenges.

Scan this QR code for a quick overview of parental recognition laws by state.

Divorce planning makes a great wedding gift! It's important to be proactive and plan for any potential financial challenges that may arise. Here are some tips to prepare for any financial situation with your spouse. These can be helpful even if you don't anticipate your relationship ending in divorce.

- Prepare and implement pre-nuptial and post-nuptial agreements with your partner before marriage.
- Understand your accounts, assets, and properties.

- Know where important documents are (titles, 401k, banks, assets, etc.).
- Make copies of all financial account information and statements for individually titled and jointly titled assets.
- Understand your rights regarding Social Security benefits and retirement account assets.
- Educate yourself on your state's current LGBTQ+ divorce and relationship recognition laws.
- Include your financial professional, attorney, and accountant in discussions about your assets.
- Regularly check your finances and make changes as needed to stay financially secure as a couple.

Know what happens to you if your partner or spouse dies. Does a pension stop? Will you lose a big Social Security check? Is there life insurance to claim? Do you need to retitle assets? Update beneficiaries? Probate a will?

BOTTOM LINE

PRIDE & PROTECTION: THE IMPORTANCE OF INSURANCE

LGBTQ+ health disparities are off-the-chart:

- 65% of LGBTQ+ adults in the US report facing discrimination in their everyday lives —double the rate of their straight counterparts.[15]
- In healthcare, one in three LGBTQ+ people report experiencing negative interactions compared to 15% of straight/cis adults.[16]

Also affecting the overall health challenges LGBTQ+ adults face, they are twice as likely to have experienced homelessness, with pronounced disparities among Black and lower-income individuals. Mental health disparities are also stark.

All of this points to the need for LGBTQ+ individuals to ensure that their financial plans include comprehensive health insurance coverage.

Let's discuss the types of coverage and why they are essential:

DISABILITY COVERAGE

We often think about standard health insurance policies, but there are other kinds of health-related insurance that everyone must consider. Short-term and long-term disability insurance are critically important while you're working, as these will help to replace your salary if there's a sickness or an accident and you can't work for a stretch of time. These plans are usually available as a group benefit. If you don't have it as a group benefit you can purchase it individually.

15,16 https://www.kff.org/racial-equity-and-health-policy/poll-finding/lgbt-adults-experiences-with-discrimination-and-health-care-disparities-findings-from-the-kff-survey-of-racism-discrimination-and-health/?utm_source=substack&utm_medium=email

CHRONIC/CRITICAL ILLNESS COVERAGE

Other types of insurance that you might be less familiar with are chronic illness and critical illness. These kinds of insurance will pay if something goes wrong. For example, critical illness is if you have cancer, a heart attack, or an organ transplant. Chronic illness is similar to long-term care insurance, where if you become disabled and chronically unable to do certain things, that insurance coverage will kick in.

here's the tea

DISCOVER THE HIDDEN BENEFITS OF A LIFE INSURANCE POLICY

A client presented his financial advisor with what he believed was a retirement savings plan he had been contributing to for years. However, a review of the policy revealed that it wasn't actually a retirement account. Instead, it was a life insurance policy that included additional riders for chronic and critical care illness.

During the review, it came to light that the client had recently been diagnosed with a form of leukemia. This diagnosis prompted a closer look at the policy's benefits. To ensure a clear understanding of the options, a call was made to the insurance company with the client present to explore whether his condition qualified for any benefits.

The discussion with the insurer revealed that the policy's chronic and critical illness riders made the client eligible for a claim due to his health status. After completing the necessary paperwork, the client received a significant payout from the policy—funds he had not known were accessible which provided much-needed financial support during a difficult time.

LIFE INSURANCE PAYOUTS

A lot of us in the LGBTQ+ community may remember during the AIDS crisis that there were viatical settlements. This was where you could sell a life insurance policy. The life insurance industry has changed to incorporate many of these benefits now in new policies that get issued. For example, there's a terminal illness rider. In the event that you are diagnosed with a terminal illness, rather than necessarily having to sell a policy, you may be able to get an advance on the death benefit.

Or, you may have a policy that you're paying into with a large death benefit, and it could be you do want to sell it. There are legitimate companies that will buy these policies. It may be a solution to stop paying premiums and benefit from the policy itself rather than leaving a death benefit to somebody who might not be as big of a priority.

MEDICARE

When I'm talking to somebody and they say, "Oh, when I turn 65 and I get Medic-Medicaid- or, no, Medicare…" and they have to think about it, that tells me plainly and quickly that they don't understand the differences. These programs are huge and so important. Everyone needs at least a basic comprehension of what applies to them and how it works.

Medicare is part of the Social Security system. You have to pay in or get married to somebody who has Medicare benefits. When you turn 65, this is going to be your health insurance, BUT, there are exceptions.

GROUP COVERAGE

If you have true group insurance — where there is a group plan of twenty or more employees — you don't necessarily have to enroll in Medicare A and B. Why wouldn't you? Medicare Part B has a premium to pay and you would be double-paying for your coverage.

If you don't have true group coverage, you do have to enroll as an individual or there is a late enrollment penalty. This is not always straightforward. For example, you may say, "Oh, I've got this plan from where I used to work, with retiree coverage." That might not count as true group coverage since you're not working there anymore. COBRA, for example, even though it comes from group coverage, does not count as true group coverage.

If you don't enroll at 65, you will get a penalty on your Medicare Part B premiums and that is a penalty for life.

Then, there's Medicare Part C (Medicare Advantage HMO/PPO) and Medicare Part D drug coverage. There's a lot to know, and it's all critically important.

C D

Scan these QR codes to take a deeper dive into understanding these other aspects of your Medicare benefit decisions.

MEDICAID

Medicaid is a form of public assistance. Eligibility is based on having very few assets and very low income. This is where people often run out of money, depending on their medical challenges and healthcare needs.

Often in planning, I am dealing with somebody—usually an older person—in a long-term care emergency. Their assets are going to be depleted. I work with an elder law attorney who will create a plan so that the person can get the Medicaid public assistance benefit for their health insurance, including possibly covering nursing home expenses.

Medicaid can be very important, but I don't want you to expect to get it without planning for it and spending down your assets.

Getting approved for Medicaid is complicated. There's a 5-year look-back, for example. You cannot simply try to plan to get this and transfer assets out. They're gonna look back five years to see if you did that and then you will not be eligible.

TRUSTS

One of the things that happens, unfortunately, is somebody may have Medicaid already, and then they inherit money which is going to blow up their health insurance. There are ways to plan for that with an eldercare attorney. You can leave the money in a trust so that it won't be counted as your asset.

LEVERAGING LONG-TERM CARE COVERAGE

I heard people say many times during COVID that we have never lived through a plague before. Well, that may be a little hard to hear for LGBTQ+ people who have dealt with the AIDS epidemic since the early 1980s. I have LGBTQ+ men as clients who are HIV+ and worry about things like health insurance options under Medicare, getting life insurance, or even long-term care insurance.

Some of the biggest concerns for many older LGBTQ+ couples, or individuals who don't have children, are questions like:

"Who's going to take care of me when I'm older and possibly alone?"

"How will my care be paid for?"

"Who's going to provide the services?"

Anxiety and uncertainty over these looming concerns as we age are definitely felt much more in the LGBTQ+ community than in the straight community. Many don't have the same family structure; many do not have children, not to the same extent. So, exploring long-term care insurance options is a key element of a comprehensive financial plan for LGBTQ+ clients.

I have gotten some HIV+ clients approved for long-term care insurance, just the same as somebody who is not HIV positive. I'm not talking about having to pay a ton extra or getting a separate/ small policy. It's the same. That's not something you're likely to come across with a financial professional who doesn't have experience dealing with the LGBTQ+ community. We have that experience and, as things change, if there are new products and insurance options for people who are HIV positive, we want to make sure that we know about it and have it available.

Another issue is that we want professionals—doctors, dentists, and specialists who are comfortable or experienced with the LGBTQ+ community — and especially within the trans community. You don't want to be in a situation where somebody is going to be judgmental when you are already in a vulnerable condition due to a health issue.

A lot of this has to do with being HIV positive, which may be a privacy issue. It's interesting, I've noticed that sometimes even those who know I'm a gay man won't mention their HIV status right away. It may be that even with me, they want to have a longer history or more of a comfort level before bringing it up. That's where it's helpful to work with somebody who's got some experience with this community.

CAREGIVING IN OUR COMMUNITY

As the LGBTQ+ community's aging population grows, it's increasingly important to ensure that all individuals have access to proper care and support. Like our straight counterparts, at some point, many of us will find ourselves in the role of caregiver for a loved one.

Especially within the LGBTQ+ community, finding caregivers and support can be particularly challenging. Factors such as financial limitations, lack of legal protections, and discrimination have created significant barriers for retired or retiring LGBTQ+ individuals.

Within gay male cultures, youth is emphasized more which often disregards aging concerns, leaving some older community members isolated, marginalized, and suffering in silence.

Entrusting the care of a loved one to a stranger can be a difficult decision—one that can be compounded by fear of inadequate treatment or discrimination for being LGBTQ+. Too often, LGBTQ+ older adults can allow this fear to postpone seeking assistance or support—which further increases isolation and decreases mental and physical health.

Let's discuss resources and solutions to overcome these challenges.

CHOSEN FAMILY CAREGIVING

Two-thirds of older LGBTQ+ adults consider their friends their chosen family.[17] Many rely on their chosen family for support, but without proper legal protections, their rights may still be jeopardized. Without written protections in place, these chosen family members will not be legally recognized and could very easily be questioned or contested by a biological family member.

17 *https://www.caregiver.org/resource/legal-issues-lgbt-caregivers/

Because many of these documents are state-specific, it is best to work with an attorney in your state when putting together advance directives and other legal documents.

here's the tea

DO YOU VALUE MY VALUES?

I hired a home health agency to take care of an older, single gay man. The agency sent a home health aide who was from a more conservative Caribbean country and culture. It is common in many parts of the USA that this work is low-paid and many employees are lower-skilled immigrants who have not had much experience with gay people in their home country. This particular aide was always reading the Bible.

We were out of the closet and making jokes. One day, she just disappeared, and they sent somebody else. We had liked her and everything was fine, but later on, we thought, you know, we scared her off.

Then we had somebody we really liked who was from Jamaica. We faced the same situation in that she came from a culturally conservative, even homophobic environment. She personally had no problem with gay people and was fantastic to work with. Years went by and one day she commented that if her husband knew that she was working with all these gay people, he'd blow a gasket.

We thought, you've got to be kidding! She had to keep quiet about us. Anti-gay attitudes exist, and gay people need to be prepared.

"GAY-GING" IN AMERICA: THE NEXT REVOLUTION

As a financial advisor who specializes in helping LGBTQ+ clients plan for retirement, I have witnessed firsthand the effects of intolerance, bullying, and systemic discrimination in housing, caregiving, and healthcare. Unfortunately, mistreatment can even come from family members, leaving many older LGBTQ+ adults vulnerable and isolated.

For LGBTQ+ older adults—especially those living with HIV—aging can present higher levels of social isolation, poverty, and inadequate access to culturally competent services compared to their straight, cisgender, and HIV-negative peers. These challenges highlight the urgent need to create safe, inclusive, and sustainable living options for our aging community.

THE SHIFTING DEMOGRAPHICS OF LGBTQ+ AGING

Today's LGBTQ+ elders are the pioneers who fought for the rights and freedoms we enjoy. They were on the frontlines during the Stonewall riots, the HIV/AIDS crisis, and the battle for marriage equality. As they age, they deserve not only our respect but also our active support in securing safe and inclusive housing solutions.

However, addressing LGBTQ+ aging isn't just about honoring our elders. We are at a generational crossroads, where the first Gen Xers are now actively planning their retirement and deciding how and where they will live in their later years. This means we must create long-term, sustainable solutions that benefit both current and future LGBTQ+ generations.

Over the next 30 years, the number of retirees in America will approach 100 million, with an estimated 5.2 million identifying as

LGBTQ+. Most LGBTQ+ older adults have no children, meaning they lack built-in family caregivers or natural heirs. In fact, more than 22 million Americans, regardless of sexual orientation, are in similar situations—needing safe, appropriate care with no immediate family to provide it. This reality necessitates innovative approaches to communal living and estate planning.

Taking Care of Our Own: Keeping Wealth in the Community

One key way to ensure LGBTQ+ older adults can age in place with dignity and proper support is by keeping financial and real estate assets within the community. By strategically planning for housing and wealth distribution, we can build a stronger foundation for LGBTQ+ aging. Here are some critical strategies:

EXPLORING NEW MODELS OF COMMUNAL LIVING

Traditional retirement communities often fail to meet the needs of LGBTQ+ individuals and couples due to discrimination or lack of cultural competency. Instead, new models of communal living offer promising alternatives:

- **Co-Housing and Shared Housing** – Living arrangements where like-minded individuals create intentional communities, sharing responsibilities, expenses, and caregiving duties.
- **Fractional Ownership** – A model where a group of LGBTQ+ individuals co-own properties, ensuring stability and mutual support in later years.
- **Intergenerational Housing** – Arrangements that bring together younger LGBTQ+ individuals with seniors, fostering mentorship, assistance, and companionship.

Donating Real Estate and Financial Assets

For those looking to leave a lasting legacy, real estate and financial planning can be powerful tools. Options include:

- **Donor-Advised Funds (DAFs)** – A philanthropic vehicle allowing individuals to allocate assets for LGBTQ+ aging initiatives and housing programs.
- **Estate Planning for Community Impact** – Ensuring assets benefit LGBTQ+ organizations, housing initiatives, or chosen family members rather than defaulting to estranged relatives or the state.

Building a Secure and Inclusive Future

Aging should be a time of security, dignity, and community—not fear and uncertainty. By investing in innovative housing solutions, communal support networks, and strategic financial planning, LGBTQ+ individuals can take control of their aging journey.

We owe it to ourselves and future generations to create a world where ALL LGBTQ+ generations can thrive. By working together, we can ensure that no one in our community has to face aging alone.

LEFT OUT OR LET IN? THE LGBTQ+ AGING DILEMMA

Although LGBTQ+ identities, relationships, and family configurations have evolved, several demographic factors still define older LGBTQ+ generations, including:

- LGBTQ+ older adults are twice as likely to be single and live alone.[18]
- Gay men tend to be less connected in friendships and partnerships[19] compared to lesbians.
- More than 1 in 3 LGBTQ+ Americans[20] report experiencing discrimination in the past year.
- LGBTQ+ older adults are four times[21] less likely to access aging services. This hesitation arises from feelings of insecurity or hostility, facing physical movement restrictions or challenges in securing transportation, and experiencing lower-quality social events.
- LGBTQ+ people of color are more vulnerable to poverty[22] and more likely to face discrimination, social stigma, and adverse health outcomes.
- Gender-expansive individuals, including transgender and non-binary people, experience fear and discrimination more than lesbian, gay, or bisexual individuals.[23]

Despite these concerning statistics, there is a strong movement in a more positive direction. With the aging of the baby boomer generation, the older adult population will rise from 16% in 2020 to an estimated 21% in 2030[24]. This solo aging wave is transforming how single seniors access financial, housing, and healthcare support.

---

18 https://www.lgbtmap.org/policy-and-issue-analysis/understanding-issues-facing-lgbt-older-adults

19 https://www.heart.org/en/news/2023/01/25/older-lgbtq-adults-face-unique-challenges-in-giving-and-receiving-care

20 https://www.americanprogress.org/article/state-lgbtq-community-2020/

21 https://www.lgbtmap.org/policy-and-issue-analysis/understanding-issues-facing-lgbt-older-adults

22 https://williamsinstitute.law.ucla.edu/publications/lgbt-poverty-us/

23 https://www.pewresearch.org/social-trends/2022/06/07/the-experiences-challenges-and-hopes-of-transgender-and-nonbinary-u-s-adults/

24 https://www.census.gov/library/stories/2018/03/graying-america.html#:~:text=Starting%20in%202030%2C%20when%20all,add%20a%20half%20million%20centenarians.

Organizations and institutions are examining every aspect of how they interact with and provide services to aging customers. More senior service and healthcare systems are providing cultural competency training to better care for LGBTQ+ seniors they serve.

Although LGBTQ+ seniors are seeing improvements in acceptance and assistance in today's society, many suffered much discrimination in their young and middle adult years. Today's older adults lived through an era that was far less tolerant of their sexuality. They had to deal with social stigma, prejudice, discrimination, and physical and verbal harassment.

For this older generation, fear of loss of employment, housing, and services if their identity was known was stressful.

For some, hiding their identity was a way to survive. Today some still hold that fear of rejection and of being ostracized by their peers.

60% of LGBTQ+ seniors hide their orientation when they enter a long-term care facility.[25] They also are less likely to seek out services like senior center events.

Once again, this pioneering generation stands at the forefront of our movement for equality, inclusion, and safety in redefining older adult housing and assisted living options.

Why is there such a demand?

LGBTQ+ older adults want a friendly living environment. As they age, many feel more vulnerable and fears of rejection, hostility, disapproval, and discrimination may grow.

We see this with some older people who are going back into the closet because they feel more vulnerable. They have to depend on other people. They depend on caregivers, and maybe an assisted living

---

25 "LGBTQ Elders Fear Being Shoved in Closet in Nursing Care Hunt", Bloomberg Law, June 28, 2022. https://news.bloomberglaw.com/social-justice/gay-elders-fear-being-shoved-back-in-closet-in-nursing-care-hunt

facility staff. Of course, they're making new friends in a place where they've moved for independent or assisted living; they don't want to get into fights or disagreements. This prompted another sailor to go back into the closet and keep their mouth shut.

A lot of older people are generally more conservative. It's a generational issue. Unlike younger people, who are so used to being out, a lot of older people are still uncomfortable. That is probably why some of these facilities are less welcoming to LGBTQ+ individuals, because they may worry that other residents might not like an openly supportive, welcoming LGBTQ+ environment.

It doesn't surprise me to hear these discrimination stories.

An older gay man shared that he was in a nice, urban, upscale assisted living facility that had regular happy hours. My husband and I had the idea of approaching the executive director to suggest that he put in the facility newsletter that there would be a gathering of LGBTQ+ people an hour earlier. We were going to be there to see if anyone else from the building would show up so we could make friendly connections.

The executive director declined the idea. There are some facilities that do want to market to the LGBTQ+ community, but others want to avoid conflict and controversy.

We see this today where large corporations are being targeted for their inclusive DEI policies, especially as it relates to the LGBTQ+ community.

Give serious thought to what you would like your living situation to be ten, twenty, and thirty years down the road. Make a plan to have the money in place and make that dream a reality.

STRENGTHENING LGBTQ+ BONDS IN LATER LIFE

There are numerous ways for older adults to expand their community connections while enhancing their mental and financial well-being:

- **Connect with local LGBTQ+ community centers** that offer drop-ins, peer-support or discussion groups, referral services, fitness programs, classes, and social activities.
- **Research inclusive housing.** 48% of LGBTQ+ couples[26] experience adverse treatment when seeking senior housing, so it's no surprise that many research inclusive housing solutions. Education on inclusivity in housing and long-term care settings—along with the growing LGBTQ+ senior population—is leading to more LGBTQ+-focused facilities and communities. Innovative housing projects by The Stonewall Community Development Corporation in New York, The Residences at Equality Park in Florida's Wilton Manors, and Mary's House in Washington, D.C. serve as models for what is possible and replicable.

26 https://endhomelessness.org/blog/housing-for-lgbtq-older-people/

Scan this QR code to learn more about innovative housing initiatives from Stonewall CDC.

- **Encourage community dialogue** to counter ageism and build understanding between LGBTQ+ generations. To see and value someone, one must hear and understand them. SAGE Table[27] is an easy-to-implement activity that doesn't require too much effort.
- **Revisit your financial plan** to ensure you are aware of your options so you can make the best decisions. Insurance requirements, healthcare needs, living situations, and legal documents change as you age. Check in with your financial advisor regularly to ensure your current and future needs are met.

ESTATE PLANNING ENSURES A HAPPY ENDING

I would say the number one issue that comes up in my financial planning discussions is missing or incomplete legal documents and end-of-life care directives.

As the COVID-19 pandemic started, my office received many calls from people who finally felt sufficiently motivated to check their beneficiaries or inquire about important legal documents such as a health care proxy, living will, power of attorney, etc.

Sometimes it takes an emergency to focus on something like this, but here's a good point: It is human nature to put off thinking about

27 https://www.sageusa.org/what-we-do/sage-table/

preparation for end-of-life, but it's important to remember that, "it's always too soon, until it's too late."

The time to have insurance is before you need it. If you don't have health insurance and have a terrible accident or sudden sickness, it's too late. If you've depended on someone else's income and that person passes away without life insurance to protect you, it's too late. If you know that you should have your legal affairs in order to protect your loved ones but you never get around to it and then something happens to you, it's too late.

Protecting yourself with specific legal documents can be exceptionally important for LGBTQ+ people, to make sure the person they have chosen has the legal right to help them, make choices for them, and possibly head off involvement from hostile relatives.

POWER OF ATTORNEY

One key document is a power of attorney (POA). Even if you're legally married, you each still need a designated power of attorney for each other.

For example, if your spouse is in the hospital or incapacitated and you have to manage the financial affairs, you are not allowed to withdraw money from his or her IRA without a power of attorney. It doesn't matter that you are married; you still need to have a power of attorney. The POA can be for financial affairs, medical issues, or both. A POA gives the person that you name the ability to make decisions for you, to access accounts, and/or to help you get medical care.

WILLS & TRUSTS

When people think of estate planning, the first thing they often think of is a will. A will is where you can direct who receives your property or assets that don't already have a named beneficiary. I prefer for as much of your property as possible to pass outside of a will. You can do this by naming a beneficiary (life insurance, retirement accounts, bank accounts), by having the assets titled so your beneficiary already has ownership.

Or, you may put assets into a revocable living trust and then those assets pass to beneficiaries according to the trust and not the will. If most of your assets are set up like this, you might not even need a will, or if you have a will, it might not need to be probated if all assets are otherwise accounted for.

ADVANCED HEALTHCARE DIRECTIVES

Advanced healthcare directives are typically a living will or a medical power of attorney. A living will is a strange name, but that's the "pull the plug" document.

Until you've gone through it, you don't know how important these documents can be. I've been through it with my own family and helped my brother to make those intense and deeply personal decisions.

Do we pull the plug?

Should I authorize a feeding tube?

Should I authorize a ventilator?

BENEFICIARIES & TITLING

It is essential to make sure that your beneficiaries are up to date. People don't always think of this but it is imperative to double-check. You may think you've got a spousal benefit, that because you are married, assets will automatically go to your husband or wife, but that is not necessarily the case. If you've got somebody else listed, perhaps an ex-spouse, or maybe a sibling from a time when you were not married, or it could be that nobody's listed, then it goes to your estate.

Proper titling of accounts is crucial. Often there is a liquidity problem after someone passes away and all assets are tied up in the estate. If you have your accounts titled properly, money can be transferred quickly. It gets very technical and the laws keep changing—particularly on IRAs or retirement accounts. It used to be that you could stretch out the required minimum distributions over a lifetime. If it's a non-spouse beneficiary, they have to be liquidated over the course of ten years.

This is a key difference between spouses and non-spouses. If you are legally married, your spouse has the right to your IRA, to receive it as though it were always his or her own. That's a key marital benefit.

GUARDIANSHIP

What can happen if you don't have a power of attorney?

You can end up being the victim of guardianship. I say victim because this seldom seems to work out well. If nobody has the right to make decisions for you and you can't make decisions for yourself, there may be a petition for guardianship. The court steps in and appoints someone. It could be a hostile relative who seeks this. This is a danger for LGBTQ+ people. It could be that you've got a mother who wants to take away a son from a same-sex partner. When that happens, the court can take away your rights and appoint them to the guardian. That includes the right to move you and to decide where you live. It can be dehumanizing. It can also be expensive, not just for the guardian services, but also for legal fees.

You want to make sure you've got a power of attorney because the courts typically look for the least restrictive alternative. They will typically go ahead and honor a power of attorney rather than appoint somebody else.

There's one other document. You can get a pre-need guardian, where you name someone to be your guardian 'if necessary'. However, if you have a power of attorney, you don't need that assuming that the power of attorney is still available and willing.

here's the tea

WHEN LIFE DOESN'T FOLLOW YOUR PLAN

A same-sex couple had been together for over twenty years. There was a noticeable age difference between them and they assumed that the older gentleman would likely pass away first. With this expectation, they focused on planning for that scenario.

However, life took an unexpected turn when the younger man passed away suddenly. Unfortunately, their estate and property plans had not been properly set up to handle this unforeseen event. The couple owned their home through a limited liability company (LLC) and they had named the deceased partner's nephew as the managing member—essentially making him the legal owner of the property upon his uncle's death. As a result, the surviving partner no longer had any legal claim to the home he had shared with his partner for decades.

Things quickly spiraled from bad to worse. A cousin of the deceased partner got involved and had the water service to the house disconnected, leaving the surviving partner without basic utilities. The situation grew dire, and the older gentleman faced the possibility of losing his home entirely.

The surviving partner sought legal help and consulted with an attorney who specialized in LGBTQ+ estate planning. Upon reviewing the case, the attorney delivered devastating news: the older gentleman had no legal right to stay in his own home. It wasn't even a matter of being evicted; he was facing an "ejection," a more severe legal action that would force him to leave immediately.

The realization of what had happened was overwhelming. The older man had always believed that after so many years together, his rights as a partner were secure. The look on his face when the attorney explained his position was heartbreaking—he never imagined that he could lose his home, especially under these circumstances. He shared that he never thought he would end up in such a vulnerable position, and it was a sobering moment for him.

This story is a reminder of how critical it is to have comprehensive estate and property plans in place, especially for LGBTQ+ couples who may face unique legal challenges. It's human nature to believe that life will follow a certain path, but unexpected events can upend even the best-laid plans. Properly structured legal documents could have prevented this situation by ensuring that the surviving partner retained ownership rights, regardless of which partner passed away first. A well-prepared estate plan is not only a financial tool—it's a crucial part of protecting people and the life they have built together.

Ask yourself when you're thinking about assigning a power of attorney or mapping out your entire estate plan …

Is this really that important?

Will this cost a lot of money?

The answer is YES. It's worth spending money on a good estate planning attorney who will do this for you so documents will not be challenged. Or, if they are challenged, having an attorney involved ensures that a challenge fails.

Any estate planning attorney is going to have horror stories about documents not being done properly or people coming out of the woodwork to cause trouble. This is why LGBTQ+ people need to work with an LGBTQ+-allied estate planning attorney.

Let's say you've got all of your legal documents completed and your end-of-life wishes written. What's the next step?

Secure legal documents in a safe place like a safe deposit box or on your password-protected personal computer, right?

No. Those are actually the worst possible places for those documents. They may not be available to the right person when that person needs them, unless they're actually listed as co-owner of the safe deposit box or have access to your passwords.

There are e-storage systems where you can upload copies of important documents and input account information, write out your wishes, and name "deputies" to receive those documents at the right time. You want to "leave a trail of breadcrumbs" so that those you have asked to help you will have any required information when they need it.

For writing and sharing your end-of-life wishes, there is a wonderfully comprehensive resource called The Conversation Project, which is dedicated to helping individuals start conversations with family and friends about what matters most to them—and to make sure they get the care they want.

Scan this QR code to access free planning guides from The Conversation Project.

Scan this QR code to access free planning guides from The Conversation Project.

In a relationship where one spouse or partner is much older than the other–particularly if it is a man, there is an assumption that the older person will pass away first. While this is likely true, don't let your whole future depend on it. It could be the opposite outcome, and what then? What does the older surviving spouse do? You MUST plan for any scenario because we cannot predict or control the future.

BOTTOM LINE

EMPOWER YOUR LGBTQ+ MONEY: INVEST TO IGNITE CHANGE

Imagine stepping into a world where your money not only secures your future but also ignites change for a better world.

That's the power of LGBTQ+ investing—to make a difference while securing your financial well-being.

Empowerment for LGBTQ+ individuals and couples parallels the journey women have undertaken over the years. It's about taking control, having confidence, and feeling secure. When you empower yourself financially, you're not just securing your own future; you're also contributing to the advancement of LGBTQ+ rights and representation in the financial world.

BARRIERS, BEHAVIORS & BIASES, OH MY!

In my practice, the number one thing I find people often need beyond a financial plan is confidence-building, emotional support, and accountability to their own money.

I ask questions like:

- Are you saving enough?
- Are you overspending?
- Are you getting into debt?
- Are you risking disaster by not having the right insurance?
- Are you trying to retire too early?
- Are you taking Social Security too early?
- Are you overlooking what could go wrong?

Fraud, business failure, divorce, disability, natural disaster, an economic meltdown, and as we have learned—even a pandemic, are just a few unexpected situations to plan for.

Many psychological elements go way beyond what you might think a financial advisor normally does. I sometimes also act as a coach and therapist.

As an advisor, I am trained to look at financial markets and decisions objectively, so I can guide my clients through negative emotional reactions such as fear, shame, or greed that may come up when discussing—or avoiding discussing—money.

This anxiety-heightening atmosphere can affect your ability to make rational financial decisions.

In addition, attitudes toward money also play into financial security, or lack of it.

Money Behaviors

Consider this list of money behaviors and think about which affect how you make important financial decisions. Do any of these describe you?

Money Silence — Let's not talk about it.

Money Shame — having feelings and making statements like …

- I'm ashamed of my debt.
- I haven't saved enough.
- I have made stupid mistakes.
- I have loaned money I am never going to get back.
- I can't seem to control my spending.

The self-shaming list goes on and on …

- Contagious Attitudes — "everyone does it" — such as taking student loans, keeping up with the Joneses, or feeling like you've got to have crypto or the hottest meme stocks
- Avoiding Unpleasant Topics – ESPECIALLY extremely unpleasant and unlikely yet potentially ruinous things, like disability or premature death

- Living For Now — paying too much attention to the present and not your future.
- Underestimating Your Longevity —probably the top blind spot people have when planning enough income to last throughout retirement.
- Sticking with a Losing Game —This is the tendency to continue a course of action even when stopping it would be more beneficial. After investing time, energy, and/or money, you may feel that it would all be for nothing if you quit, so you continue throwing good money after bad. This only compounds the mistake.
- Bad Decisions — making bad decisions and/or non-decisions.
- Needs vs. Wants — Can you spot the difference between what you want and what you require?

My clients always answer "yes" to at least one of these behaviors. There is no guilt or shame in owning up to them. Admitting this is the first step in letting them go.

What's important is recognizing how they have affected your financial goals so you can change. Adjust your money behaviors to empower yourself and make healthier decisions moving forward.

Confirmation Bias

Another question to ask yourself is do you have any confirmation bias that might cloud your judgment or keep you from making fully-informed decisions?

For example, take someone listening to a colleague who is bragging about the latest hot stock. They may feel anxious about missing out and decide to do some research on their own.

As they search the internet for validation, their mind may be picturing the possible impact of this stock and how they may be perceived if they don't get in on the deal.

This person may let fear and greed creep into their research process, which could affect their ability to spot red flags or stick to their planned investment strategy.

Confirmation bias works subtly inside the minds of people striving to make decisions that bring them closer to their goals. Even in people who spend time analyzing the cons as well as the pros of a decision, confirmation bias may give more weight to the pros if there is a preconception in favor of it.

To put it simply, confirmation bias may cause us to discredit information that doesn't align with and support our beliefs. This is a potentially harmful mindset where finances are concerned.

Overcoming confirmation bias doesn't necessarily mean abandoning preconceived opinions; it means recognizing how bias may lead to making harmful decisions in any aspect of your life.

When gathering and analyzing information, try to find opinions that don't conform to your beliefs, then aim to understand why. This may involve inviting people who don't share your views to give you their thoughts without arguing yours. Just listen and evaluate.

The same can be done by reading articles by people with different opinions.

Trying to work through the thought process rationally without fighting opposing views is a good place to start.

ESG & DEI: LGBTQ+ VALUES IN ACTION

ESG stands for Environmental, Social, and Governance investments.[28]

---

28 ESG investing involves the exclusion of certain securities for non-financial reasons. This may result in the investor forgoing some market opportunities that may have been available to those not subject to such criteria. There is no guarantee that any investment goal will be met.

It's becoming more crucial than ever to address some of the world's most pressing challenges, to ensure a sustainable future for people and our planet, including:

- Climate risk and returns
- Environmental regulations
- Corporate transparency

And, of special interest for us in the LGBTQ+ community ...

- Promoting diversity, equity, and inclusion (DEI)
- Protecting human rights

DEI initiatives and investments were the hot thing in corporate America a few years ago. Now? Not so much.

Today, the business community—long averse to political risks or controversies is backing away from DEI programs in the wake of executive orders from President Trump and widespread attacks from Elon Musk, Bill Ackman, Stephen Miller, and federal and state lawmakers.

This indicates a significant shift in public sentiment toward these types of investments.

Some companies are changing programs designed to support women and people of color because of lawsuits—many have been filed over these programs, more than twenty by Miller's America First Legal. Other companies worry about litigation.

Companies that never cared much about DEI or fear lawsuits over programs are using the moment to back away.

Others are sticking with these efforts but doing it quietly — often changing the acronym to related topics but not directly stating they are DEI.

The ESG Landscape: A Rollercoaster Ride

In 2021, the ESG sector experienced substantial growth, with inflows reaching $70 billion.

And, like DEI initiatives, politics have changed how people talk about ESG.

40% of United States companies got negative feedback, so some started "greenhushing" to not talk about ESG directly.[29]

Critics have accused financial firms of prioritizing a perceived "woke" agenda over fiduciary duties, leading to a reevaluation of communication strategies and terminology.

There are many benefits to embracing an ESG investment strategy, including:

- **Ethical Investment Decisions:** You have the opportunity to make ethical investment decisions that resonate with your personal values. ESG criteria allow you to evaluate the behavior of companies beyond their financial performance, ensuring that your investments support businesses that prioritize sustainability, responsible governance, and positive societal impact.
- **Promoting Positive Change:** When investors demand transparency, ethical conduct, and sustainability, businesses are incentivized to adapt their behaviors and practices to these values.
- **Mitigating Risks:** Companies with strong ESG scoring performance are often better prepared to manage risks, whether they are related to environmental challenges, labor disputes, governance issues, or regulatory changes. Investing in such companies can help you mitigate potential risks in your investment portfolio.

---

29 https://www.weforum.org/agenda/2022/11/what-is-greenhushing-and-is-it-really-a-cause-for-concern/

- **Long-Term Sustainability:** Sustainable investments are focused on the long term. Companies that embrace ESG principles tend to be more resilient in the face of economic downturns or market fluctuations. Their strong ethical foundations often translate into stable financial performance, making them attractive choices for investors with a long-term perspective.
- **Investor Satisfaction:** Fostering a sense of connection between your wealth and your values can bring a profound sense of satisfaction and purpose.
- **Attracting Responsible Investors:** Investing with ESG principles can attract like-minded investors. This can lead to greater demand for ESG-conscious investments, potentially driving up their value and creating a more vibrant market for ethical investments. Increased interest from investors is fueling fast track ESG in just about every corner of the business world.
- **Regulatory and Market Trends:** Governments, stock exchanges, and financial institutions are promoting responsible investment practices. Investing in line with these trends can result in favorable treatment and opportunities, such as better access to capital and enhanced market presence.

The challenge lies in balancing social impact goals with financial returns. While some social impact investments may offer competitive returns, others may prioritize societal benefits over financial gain. It's essential to clearly define your objectives and ensure your chosen investments align with them.

Whether through ESG-focused mutual funds, green bonds, or community development funds, there are various avenues to invest in initiatives that support the LGBTQ+ community.

CONFESSIONS OF A CLIENT WHISPERER

There is so much negativity out there. Anxiety and concern about the financial markets, wealth disparity, inflation, uncivil politics, loss of human rights like limited abortion access and anti-LGBTQ+ legislation, climate change, gun violence, and deep uncertainty about our country's future.

It's one thing after another.

And it's really affecting people.

It is affecting me.

Negative emotions can fool us the most. Negative perspectives are misleading, and I am here to tell you that you don't need to give in to them.

I don't want to minimize the serious things happening in the world, but none of us has control over these larger economic and societal issues.

What you DO have, however, is freedom to make positive decisions that help you live your best life.

I make a conscious effort every day to focus on the positive ways I can help my clients; sharing resources and solutions to empower and inspire them.

As a financial advisor, I have investment options that address and reduce fear and worry.

There are money managers—and we work with them—who will reduce risk automatically by getting out of the market and going to cash—meaning they will sell off stock market investments and convert them to money, to minimize losses. This may give you more financial confidence.

We also plan and prepare for other risks based on your feedback, concerns, and risk tolerance. This may include putting less money in the market, or selecting more conservative or guaranteed investments.

It's important to keep in mind that historically, the market has ups and downs. It's just a fact that financial markets rise and fall—and always will. Volatility and market corrections are part of the equation.

My job is to ensure you plan for all types of market conditions, to minimize risk and have your portfolio meet your needs in the long run.

In the event of a setback or downturn, there are always money management solutions to get you back on the right path.

Getting back on a healthier financial path amidst uncertainty in other aspects of life takes mindful effort.

I am committed to sharing my perspectives and recommendations based on decades of experience, to help you move forward informed, prepared, empowered, and living confidently with positive intentions.

It is okay to not feel OK about everything … but trust that you have the power to live your best life despite what's happening in the larger world.

Just knowing that can make a big difference.

WHAT'S YOUR MONEY MANTRA?

We've explored the psychological and emotional factors of your relationship to money, and how various money behaviors can affect your financial health.

I hope you've gained a deeper understanding of your emotional triggers and identified one or more money behaviors that you will focus on changing.

I leave you with one assignment …

Create your own personal money mantra that speaks to your financial goals.

For example, if you're worried about making a big financial decision, stop and ask yourself: "Would my advisor approve of this?"

ABOUT THE AUTHOR

David Treece is a fearless financial advocate for the LGBTQ+ community.

David believes it's not enough to say, "I treat everybody the same," because everyone is NOT the same. As a gay-identified financial advisor, he understands LGBTQ+ individuals' real-world apprehension and mistrust toward the historically conservative financial industry.

David has provided advocacy-oriented financial advice and service to South Florida's LGBTQ+ community for almost four decades. At the forefront of his work is navigating the sometimes complex financial and healthcare needs of LGBTQ+ individuals as they age, oftentimes alone without a strong support network.

He is a national leader in educating financial advisors on understanding LGBTQ+ clients' unique issues when it comes to financial and life-planning.

Beyond financial planning, David is the founder and first president of the Greater Miami LGBTQ+ Chamber of Commerce and has been honored by The National LGBTQ+ Task Force for his contribution to advancing full freedom, justice, and equality for LGBTQ+ people.

Recognized for his financial acumen and client-advocacy work, David has been featured on PBS's *Nightly Business Report, Q News Tonight,* and *NBC Miami,* as well as in *The Washington Post, The Miami Herald* and nationally-syndicated columns.

David holds life, health, and annuity insurance licenses as well as series 6, 22, 52 62, 63, and 65 securities registrations. He also has an MBA from the University of Michigan, Ann Arbor. He and Luis, his husband of forty years, divide their time between South Florida and San Antonio de Areco, Argentina.

David Treece
President, Treece Financial Group Inc.
Investment Advisor Representative
AIF® Accredited Investment Fiduciary
CLTC® Certification in Long-Term Care
Founder, La Vida Pride™ LGBTQ+ eCommunity

Treece Financial Group Inc.
7971 Riviera Blvd., Suite 331
Miramar, FL 33023
(305) 751-8855
info@davidtreece.com
TreeceFi.com

www.ingramcontent.com/pod-product-compliance
Lightning Source LLC
LaVergne TN
LVHW051054210926
848486LV00002B/108
9798349336126